The Lord bless you and keep you;
The Lord make His face shine upon you,
And be gracious to you;
The Lord lift up His countenance upon you,
And give you peace.

~ Numbers 6:24-26

For the preaching of the cross
is to them that perish foolishness;
but unto us which are saved
it is the power of God.

~ 1 Corinthians 1:18

Barbershop Ministries
30-Day Journal
for
Prayer
&
Meditating
on the Word

Michael Luther
Pentecostal Preacher (Ordained)

With

shELAH
yOur BackYard Publishing

© 2020
Publisher: yOur BackYard Publishing
Centerville TN 37033
USA

Editor: shELAH
ybymedia@gmail.com

Introduction

In memory of Dr. Clifford Reynolds, best friend and pastor for more than 40 years.

I pray that the verses in this book not only bless and encourage you, the reader, but also motivate you to memorize more Bible verses... to hide more and more of God's word in your heart.

Search
from the book
of the Lord
and read.
~ Isaiah 34:16a

Behold,
a virgin shall be with child,
and shall bring forth a son,
and they shall call his name
Emmanuel,
which being interpreted is,
God with us.

~ Matthew 1:23

Therefore
the Lord himself
shall give you a sign;
Behold, a virgin shall conceive,
and bear a son,
and shall call his name
Immanuel.

~ Isaiah 7:14

Moreover, brethren,
I declare unto you the gospel
which I preached unto you,
which also ye have received,
and wherein ye stand;
By which also ye are saved...
For I delivered unto you first of all
that which I also received,
how that Christ died for our sins
according to the scriptures;
And that he was buried,
and that he rose again the third day
according to the scriptures:

~ 1 Corinthians 15:1-4

Beloved, believe not every spirit,
but try the spirits
whether they are of God:
because many false prophets
are gone out into the world.
Hereby know ye the Spirit of God:
Every spirit that confesseth
that Jesus Christ is come in the flesh
is of God:
And every spirit that confesseth not
that Jesus Christ is come in the flesh
is not of God:
and this is that spirit of antichrist,
whereof ye have heard
that it should come;
and even now
already is it in the world.
Ye are of God, little children,
and have overcome them:
because greater is he that is in you,
than he that is in the world.

~ 1 John 4:1-4

Not every one that saith unto me,
Lord, Lord,
shall enter into the kingdom of heaven;
but he that doeth the will of my Father
which is in heaven.
Many will say to me in that day,
Lord, Lord,
have we not prophesied in thy name?
and in thy name
have cast out devils?
and in thy name
done many wonderful works?
And then will I profess unto them,
I never knew you:
depart from me,
ye that work iniquity.

~ Matthew 7:21-23

For all have sinned,
and come short
of the glory of God;

~ Romans 3: 23

Then Peter said unto them,
Repent, and be baptized every one of you
in the name of Jesus Christ f
or the remission of sins,
and ye shall receive
the gift of the Holy Ghost.

~ Acts 2:38

Jesus answered
and said unto him,
Verily, verily,
I say unto thee,
Except a man
be born again,
he cannot see
the kingdom of God.

~ John 3:3

...if thou shalt confess with thy mouth
the Lord Jesus,
and shalt believe in thine heart
that God hath raised him from the dead,
thou shalt be saved.
For with the heart
man believeth unto righteousness;
and with the mouth
confession is made unto salvation.
For the scripture saith,
Whosoever believeth on him
shall not be ashamed.
For there is no difference
between the Jew and the Greek:
for the same Lord over all
is rich unto all
that call upon him.
For whosoever shall call
upon the name of the Lord
shall be saved.

~ Romans 10:9-13

For by grace
are ye saved
through faith;
and that not of yourselves:
it is the gift of God:
Not of works,
lest any man should boast.

~ Ephesians 2:8-9

There is therefore now
no condemnation to them
which are in Christ Jesus,
who walk not after the flesh,
but after the Spirit.

~ Romans 8:1

For God sent not his Son
into the world to condemn the world;
but
that the world
through him
might be saved.

~ John 3:17

Then Agrippa said unto Paul,
Almost
thou persuadest me
to be a Christian.

~ Acts 26:28

"Almost is not enough...."

In Remembrance
of the late
Rev. Michael Whobrey

In 1983, "Mike" First Preached
the Sermon,
"Almost is not enough...,"
in
Dickson, Tennessee

> But he that shall blaspheme*
> against the Holy Ghost
> hath never forgiveness,
> but is in danger
> of eternal damnation:
>
> ~ Mark 3:29

To those who like Agrippa may almost be persuaded:

*As John 3: 18 notes, you who do not believe in Christ are condemned. No matter how good you try to be or how many good works you do, your unbelief, a state of sin without Christ, makes you guilty before God. When you say that you reject Christ, you express a condition of your heart.

Dr. J. Vernon McGee explains that the unpardonable sin depicts the willful, voluntary "refusal to accept the pardon God offers by the convicting work of the Holy Spirit." When the Holy Spirit convicts a person and draws them to Christ, that person makes a choice; to accept the forgive- ness and eternal life that Jesus Christ died on the cross to offer or reject Jesus. They can choose an eternity without God by rejecting [blaspheming] the Holy Spirit until He no longer strives with them.

By this
shall all men know
that ye are my disciples,
if
ye have love one to another.

~ John 13:35

He who does not love
does not know God,
for God is love.

~ 1 John 4:8

For this is the love of God,
that we keep his commandments:
and his commandments
are not grievous.

~ 1 John 5:3

Charity [Love] suffereth* long,
and is kind;
charity envieth not;
charity vaunteth not itself,
is not puffed up,
Doth not behave itself unseemly,
seeketh not her own,
is not easily provoked, thinketh no evil;
Rejoiceth not in iniquity,
but rejoiceth in the truth;
Beareth all things, believeth all things,
hopeth all things,
endureth all things.

~ 1 Corinthians 13:4-8

*to be of a long spirit, not to lose heart
G3114 μακροθυμέω makrothymeō

And as it is appointed unto men
once to die,
but after this the judgment:

~ Hebrews 9:27

It is a fearful thing
to fall
into the hands of the living God.

~ Hebrews 10:31

And we have seen and do testify
that the Father sent the Son
to be the Saviour of the world.
Whosoever shall confess that
Jesus is the Son of God,
God dwelleth in him, and he in God.
And we have known and believed
the love that God hath to us.
God is love;
and he that dwelleth in love
dwelleth in God, and God in him.
Herein is our love made perfect,
that we may have boldness
in the day of judgment:
because as he is,
so are we in this world.
There is no fear in love;
but perfect love casteth out fear:
because fear hath torment.
He that feareth
is not made perfect in love.
We love him,
because he first loved us.

~ John 4:14-18

Blessed is the man
that walketh not
in the counsel of the ungodly,
nor standeth in the way of sinners,
nor sitteth in the seat of the scornful.
But his delight
is in the law of the Lord;
and in his law
doth he meditate day and night.
And he shall be
like a tree
planted by the rivers of water,
that bringeth forth his fruit
in his season;
his leaf also shall not wither;
and whatsoever he doeth
shall prosper.

~ Psalm 1:1-3

Honour the Lord with thy substance,
and with the firstfruits
of all thine increase:

~ Proverbs 3:9

Give, and it shall be given unto you;
good measure, pressed down,
and shaken together, and running over,
shall men give into your bosom.
For with the same measure
that ye mete withal
it shall be measured to you again.

~ Luke 6:38

But seek ye first the kingdom of God,
and his righteousness;
and all these things
shall be added unto you.

~ Matthew 6:33

Know ye not,
that to whom ye yield yourselves
servants to obey,
his servants ye are to whom ye obey;
whether of sin unto death,
or of obedience unto righteousness?

~ Romans 6:16

For the kingdom of God
is not meat and drink;
but righteousness, and peace,
and joy in the Holy Ghost.

Romans 14:17

After this manner therefore, pray ye:
Our Father which art in heaven,
Hallowed be thy name.
Thy kingdom come.
Thy will be done in earth,
as it is in heaven.
Give us this day our daily bread.
And forgive us our debts,
as we forgive our debtors.
And lead us not into temptation,
but deliver us from evil one.
For thine is the kingdom
and the power
and the glory, for ever.
Amen.

~Matthew 6:9-13

Jesus said that...

...Eye has not seen,
nor ear heard,
Nor have entered
into the heart of man
The things which God
has prepared
for those who love Him.

~ 1 Corinthians 2:9

...be strong in the Lord
and in the power of his might.
Put on the whole armour of God,
that ye may be able to stand
against the wiles of the devil.
For we do not wrestle against
flesh and blood,
but against principalities,
against powers,
against the rulers
of the darkness of this world,
against spiritual hosts of wickedness
in the high places.

~ Ephesians 6:10–12

If my people,
which are called by my name,
shall humble themselves,
and pray,
and seek my face,
and turn from their wicked ways;
then will I hear from heaven,
and will forgive their sin,
and will heal their land.

~ 2 Chronicles 7:14

Wherefore take unto you
the whole armour of God,
that ye may be able
to withstand in the evil day,
and having done all, to stand.
Stand therefore,
having your loins girt
about with truth, and having on
the breastplate of righteousness;
And your feet shod
with the preparation
of the gospel of peace;

~ Ephesians 6:13–15

Above all, taking the shield of faith,
wherewith ye shall be able
to quench
all the fiery darts of the wicked.
And take the helmet of salvation,
and the sword of the Spirit,
which is the word of God:
Praying always with all prayer
and supplication in the Spirit,

~ Ephesians 6:16–18a

The Spirit of the Lord is upon me,
because he hath anointed me
to preach the gospel to the poor;
he hath sent me
to heal the brokenhearted,
to preach deliverance
to the captives,
and recovering of sight
to the blind,
to set at liberty
them that are bruised,

~ Luke 4:18

Serve the Lord with gladness:
come before his presence with singing.
Know ye that the Lord he is God:
it is he that hath made us,
and not we ourselves;
we are his people,
and the sheep of his pasture.
Enter into his gates with thanksgiving,
and into his courts with praise:
be thankful unto him,
and bless his name.
For the Lord is good;
his mercy is everlasting;
and his truth endureth
to all generations.

~ Psalm 100:2-5

Let not your heart be troubled:
ye believe in God,
believe also in me.
In my Father's house
are many mansions:
if it were not so,
I would have told you.
I go to prepare a place for you.
And if I go
and prepare a place for you,
I will come again,
and receive you unto myself;
that where I am,
there ye may be also.

~ John 14:1-3

Jesus said that....

...As your days,
so shall your strength be.

~ Deuteronomy 33:25b

For God so loved the world,
that he gave his only begotten Son,
that whosoever believeth in him
should not perish,
but have everlasting life.
For God sent not his Son into the world
to condemn the world;
but that the world through him
might be saved.
He that believeth on him
is not condemned:
but he that believeth not
is condemned already,
because he hath not believed
in the name of
the only begotten Son of God.

~ John 3:16-18

But these are written,
that ye might believe
that Jesus is the Christ,
the Son of God;
and that believing
ye might have life
through his name.
~ John 20:31

Behold, I stand at the door, and knock:
if any man hear my voice, and open the door,
I will come in to him,
and will sup with him,
and he with me.

~ Revelation 3:20

www.ingramcontent.com/pod-product-compliance
Lightning Source LLC
Chambersburg PA
CBHW071540080526
44588CB00011B/1732